THIS SKETCHBOOK BELONGS TO ....

CONTACT ....